A Day In An Elephant's Life

A Rhyming Story

By Rhonda Ragland

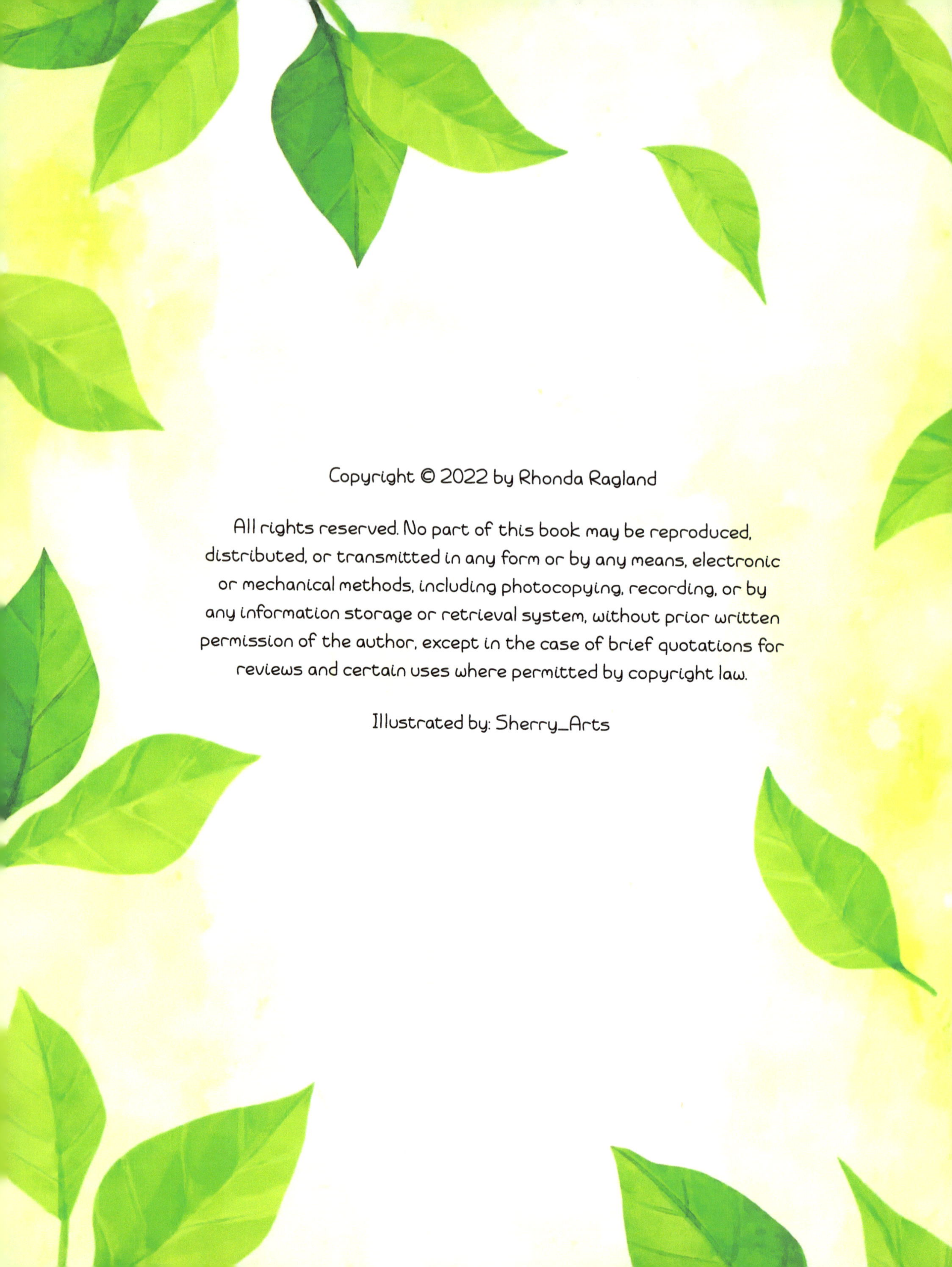

Illustrated by: Sherry_Arts

This book is dedicated to my children for
all the cherished memories of rhyming
and elephant drawings. I love you.

A day in an elephant's life filled with fun,
Adventure, exploring, and love a ton.
Journeying through the jungle, one by one,
The adventure starts with the rising sun.

Molly and Milo are little sister and brother,
The little elephants stay close to their mother.

The three of them have the best of times together,
Every day is an adventure, no matter the weather.

Mom always makes sure they do not stray too far away,
And she watches Molly and Milo closely as they play.
The little elephants love to play and run around,
They dance and trumpet their signature sound.

11

Today, the elephants go past the trees and beyond,
They walk and walk until they find a tiny pond.
Mom makes sure it is safe to get wet,
No scary lions or crocodiles to fret.

Looking around, Mom counts to ten,
Knowing it is safe, they can now jump in.

3 4 5
2 10 6
1 9 8 7
15

Molly and Milo swim and splash each other clean,
But when they get out, they need some sunscreen.
Mom sprays dirt on Milo to cover him well,
The sun cannot reach him if he has a cool, dirt shell.

Molly says, "Here, Mom, let me help you!"
But what Molly has in mind, Mom has no clue.
Molly scoops up dirt and sprays Milo too,
Molly said, "Let's play peekaboo."

Milo runs after her, with a big smile,

They giggle and run around for a while.

Mom sprays so much dirt the kids can't take more,

And the three of them start to laugh like never before.

As they stop under a tree to get some rest,
Mom says, "Molly and Milo, you're the best,"
Together, they know to enjoy the little things,
And don't worry about what tomorrow brings.

Mom protects her children where they don't get hurt,
And sometimes they even get sprayed with dirt.

The elephants remember that it's all love,
Every day is an adventure and a gift from above.

The End